Differently Me!

Copyright 2011, 2015, 2018, 2022
Chris L McClish
Publisher: CoachCMC LLC
This lastest edition contains some small changes.

Table of Contents

Dedicated to my wife and family for supporting me all these years!

Thanks to the ACT community and the founders who inspired me to create this work!

In 2011 when this was originally published, I was unaware of any other books that applied ACT or mindfulness skills for those with high functioning autism. I am glad to have made this book to potentially have introduced these concepts to this population.

Prologue

My childhood was a mixed bag. I was sloppy at learning handwriting and started out very poor at reading. Teachers noticed I had a very large vocabulary – as most kindergarten and first grade students don't use words like "pertains to" or "nomenclature" and such. My father had me when he was sixty and my mother was forty-five, so they were considerably older than most other children's parents that I knew. My father didn't participate in teaching me any sports. I had half-brothers, but they were grown and out of the house. I felt alone. My father was restless and liked to move. We had moved 15 times in Oklahoma before moving to the Kansas City area by the time I was about ten years old.

I remember that one of my second-grade teachers suspected something was wrong with me, to my parent's defensive dismay. Yet, I was sent to Oklahoma University for testing. All I remember about my psychological testing at that age was putting together some puzzles, reading, and a lady in a suit telling my parents that I wasn't slow at all – I was "gifted". I went from feeling like the dummy in class, to being put in a gifted and talented program where I was able to learn about telescopes and watch a veterinarian dissect or do surgery on a cat! If you have heard the saying "your mother dresses you funny", it must have been true in my case as I was treated as an outsider at school. I was very shy except for some rare episodic class clown moments.

Middle school was horrible for me. My life fell apart with being tripped down the halls, having my head slammed into lockers and being called all sorts of names. I didn't party or do drugs, but it sure seemed that everyone else did. I learned how to fight, or at least I learned how to take several hits without crying or feeling more pain than I could handle. How did I get through this? I mostly lived in a fantasy world.

I would daydream about my special powers. When it was time for high school, I decided to go to a private high school to avoid further struggles.

During high school, I spent the first two years being unpopular and basically feeling like I didn't really exist in most other people's minds. With some weightlifting and literally forcing myself to talk, I became more popular by my junior and senior years – but I wouldn't have made Homecoming King by any means. I didn't participate in any sports, and still didn't attend any parties. My evenings were spent taking care of ill parents who had health issues. I did go on a few dates, but these dates were disastrous. I really didn't know how to treat females. My father was not a good role model as he was suffering from Alzheimer's and had episodes of violence, not to mention his purchasing things that we couldn't afford on impulse, leaving the burners on the stove, and other not so fun things that I don't really care to share. By senior year he was in a nursing home.

When I went off to college, one of my half-brothers died (I will not get into how it happened here). I was very close to him. My mother had several heart attacks following his death. I think she made it to seven heart attacks and at least three episodes of heart failure before she died). Everything that I had was sold in an estate sale for the care of my father- who was also dying. I lost my house – everything. So what did I do to cope? I asked a girl, that I had somehow managed to get the courage to date, if she would marry me.

My wife and I worked at a department store part-time (and other such jobs), while living in a rented-out garage, which was converted into a tiny "house" and rented to us by another half-brother. I should add that this rental "house" wasn't in the best of neighborhoods and both of us were scared. I managed to take out enough student loans to get through college, going the route of psychology and taking on jobs in the mental health field, all the while.

I need to backtrack a little. Prior to meeting my wife at a college, I had previously attended another college and learned, the hard way, the dangers of alcohol abuse, parties, etc. I was originally taking both psychology and computer programming, but hours sitting at a computer looking at code made me "want to go the easy route and do psychology".

We went through rough periods financially, and I will be the first to say I wasn't all that mentally stable. Memories of trauma and other memories of a chaotic childhood snuck into my brain at times. Bookstores were my solace. I was learning more and more on my own about eastern philosophy. It would eventually become part of my thesis that I would defend in graduate school in 1995. I had a mentor back in 1993 that also helped me learn the wonderful psychologies from the East (thanks Steve Yates.) I was reading more and more about the benefits of mindfulness and meditation. To be honest though, I didn't do so well at practicing sitting meditation, as I was way too hyper and restless to sit down for very long. I have always had a weird mix of shyness combined with a restless energy.

Mindfulness and acceptance became a way of life for me. I wouldn't be until much later, after working in the mental health field for many years, that I would repeatedly hear about psychologies becoming popular based on mindfulness that were now becoming mainstream in the United States and other western countries. Dialectic Behavioral Therapy (DBT) and Mindfulness Based Cognitive Therapy (MCBT) were some. I personally felt MCBT was too simple for my taste and DBT was way too complicated. If you are not sure about what either of those are, they are psychological approaches. Through a podcast about AD/HD (attention deficit hyperactive disorder), I heard about something called ACT or acceptance and commitment therapy. I kind of ignored it, but when I started seeing books around me, it sparked a curiosity. Opening up my first ACT books: *The Happiness Trap* by Russ Harris and *Get*

Out of Your Mind and Into Your Life by Steven C. Hayes, both validated everything that I had been doing personally and with my clients through the years. It was a perfect fit. I then began: listening, reading and flooding myself with everything there is to know about this psychological approach called ACT. I should mention that researching things to infinity is a common practice for me. Anyway, without saying too much about myself, with my Aspie mind, I have been helped personally by this practice and I have seen clients who put this into practice benefit greatly!

This is not the "be all" guide to ACT – as there is a wealth of excellent reading material on that approach for various mental (and dealing with some physical) issues. This is written for someone like me – I wanted to make it as efficient and quick to read as I could, while attempting to maintain some good content. This guide or workbook could be looked at as being a starting point self-help guide for those with "different" brains, or it can be used as a reference book for a professional working with high functioning individuals with my same type of brain wiring.

If you decide you don't like it, thank your mind for that thought and use what you can from it! - C

Chapter 1 - Do I need to change?

We have heard people tell us for many years that each individual is unique. Not everyone thinks the same, looks the same, views things the same, etc. We also are bombarded with trainings in the workplace about cultural diversity, gender differences, etc. Until recent years, little was said of a new and emerging difference to be aware of: neurodiversity. What is neurodiversity? Maybe a better way to define it would be to describe what it is and isn't and allow you to come up with your own definition.

Let's start out by talking about commonalities between average individuals. A person who is considered "normal" in the school and workplace is someone who probably wouldn't stand out if you were filming a documentary about school and career life. On websites promoted by the non-typical individual, this average conformer and linear thinking person has often been called "neurotypical". A neurotypical or "NT" would have little difficulty sitting, listening, socializing, knowing when to be quiet, and knowing when to speak. These NT individuals: dress as their peers do, are usually aware of social cues, and have little to no problem "clocking in" to work on time, no problem with functioning at school or work (like being able to sit and accomplish what needs to be done). Such a person with NT characteristics would most likely be able to readily spot someone like me: someone who is odd, whose has difficulty socializing, a strange walk, who has difficulty learning, difficulty finding the "right words" (or any words at all) and who has difficulty controlling things like attention or awareness of certain things around me.

The school environment may be the first place where a non-neurotypical would also get a label. Some of these labels are nice, some technical, and some downright mean. Overheard names for non-NT's would be names or labels such as "nerd", "geek", "strange", "hyper", "lonely", "shy", "different", "ADHD", "learning disabled", "dyslexic", "having high functioning autism", "having Asperger's Syndrome", etc.

It is not my intent to elaborate on many of the various mental disorders listed above, nor would I have you risk or attempt self-diagnosis based on this writing. If you are not sure what AD/HD, Tourette's, Autism Spectrum Disorders, etc. are, there is wealth of information available on the internet (albeit some of it inaccurate) and I think it is important for you to see a mental health professional if you have not already been diagnosed - yet are convinced that you have one of these things that society calls "disorders".

Basically, people who would be classified by doctors or other mental health professionals as being on the autistic spectrum and/or having ADHD, and those with differences in learning styles, and having poor social skills would fit into the non-neurotypical category. These atypical individuals (different, like me) often find that they are still expected to conform to the school setting or the work setting. Uniquely minded individuals, such as I, must also conform in a marriage and in social settings. If someone is not able to easily adapt and conform, relationships are often ruined (or we develop friendships and romantic relationships with others who accept us or even those who are like us). If we are aware that problems with fitting in will exist in the work setting, we hopefully (have or will) choose a career choice suited for our unique style of thinking (an artsy person would – well, go into arts or graphic arts or something). Sometimes us neurodiverse individuals may end up in a job where we fail to conform and thus frequently get into trouble for not being like the rest. However, some of us neurodiverse do end up succeeding, and become the musicians, inventors, and great minds behind many amazing accomplishments.

There are two extreme camps of thought about such individuals like me who are different. One side points to us as being "defective", "diseased", "impaired", etc. The other side points to our strengths and views us as just being "wired differently". Those who view us from the disease/impaired viewpoint may overlook the strengths, talents and accomplishments or be quick to look for a "cure" that will "rid of us" of our "disease". Those with the "wired differently" perspective may overlook some of the damage in functioning in the real world (reading, writing, socializing, making income, etc.). For those of us that are not heavily impacted adversely, I personally lean towards the "wired differently" or "different not defective viewpoint". I still recognize that my viewpoint has its limitations, as even those with mild levels of differences may not be saved from being made fun of, needing to take disability, struggling in relationships, etc. In short, I would much rather view myself and have the world view me as different rather than defective.

For those on the autistic spectrum, being "higher functioning" means that we are not what most people think of when they think of autism, which would be those on the lower functioning end. Some people may even think of savants like "Rain Man" when they think of autism. Those of us with higher functioning may look and may even act (around others most of the time) "normal". I should point out though, that being higher-functioning does not mean that we have no problems, struggles, or that we are able to handle everything in a world designed around the neurotypical individual. So, If there were a therapy to improve the lives of us non-neurotypical individuals (or those who are "neurodiverse"), what would it be?

The first intervention to assist a person like me that may jump out of a mental health professional's mind may be some sort of social skills training. I do believe it may help to train and work on social skills and other such life skills with someone with higher functioning autism or other disorders which impact communication, in which type of therapy, the professional would teach us how to read social cues, make use of eye contact effectively, and use other resources. Likewise, a person with AD/HD may benefit by organization skills, memory techniques, etc. Having a coach and learning a few skills may make some noticeable differences (or save a job, marriage, etc.).

If there is depression involved (and often there is) a type of therapy known as cognitive behavioral therapy may come to mind. This therapeutic approach is designed to assist a client in identifying and replacing negative "self talk" or messages that he or she has internalized about failings, frustrations, differences, etc. Popular recently, is DBT: dialectic behavioral therapy – which would add mindfulness with a cognitive behavioral therapeutic approach as well as some skills to handle emotions, boundaries, etc.

I have another preference from a psychological reference point. Being a fan of mindfulness and Eastern theory, as well as my background for many years with those with addictions, I highly value the idea behind the Serenity Prayer: "Grant me the serenity to accept the things I can not change, the courage to change the things that I can, and the wisdom to know the difference [by Reinhold Niebuhr]. A psychotherapeutic approach that contains elements of the wisdom of the serenity prayer, is a form of behaviorism developed by Steven C. Hayes and others, known as Acceptance and Commitment Therapy or "ACT" for short. ACT, pronounced like the word, not the initials, was based off of something called relational frame theory (very technical, so I will not even touch the definition here). There have been studies that demonstrate how ACT is effective with people from various backgrounds and effective in helping with many disorders. It is beyond the scope of this writing, for me to discuss ACT in great detail. I also wanted this writing to be based off clinical and experiential conclusions (I don't want this to be too scientific) – therefore, you will not see me citing research studies or feeling the need to back up my conclusions with footnotes. There are good books on ACT if you would like more information. The concepts contained in these pages are derived from ACT founders and those in the ACT community such as Steven Hayes, Kelly G. Wilson, Kirk Strosahl, Russ Harris, and a few more (including the ACT online community). In summary, I like ACT for this approach's emphasis on acceptance, mindfulness, commitment to change, moving toward values, and most importantly, ACT therapists not seeing clients as being defective or damaged goods.

Anyway, I hope now you have (or already had) an idea of what neurodiversity is. If we could train schools and organizations to understand that not everyone responds well to the same type of learning style, grading system, social setting, etc., then we - as a society - may help individuals with these types of characteristics not feel rejected. Until that time, "it is what it is" for those of us who need to function in a world that caters to the neurotypical. So, I want to spend time with you, the reader, talking about moving forward despite your differences from mainstream society. Call yourself an "Aspie", "ADD'er" or whatever label(s) that you or the professionals have given you but, please, don't see yourself as being a mistake or defective. From this point forward, I may use the initials NT to represent the neurotypical individual and ND to represent those of us who are on the spectrum, or have AD/HD, or a learning disorder (or the ND can represent anyone who considers himself to just think function "differently").

Oh, I forgot something (I tend to forget things easily). I am providing you with some concepts from the psychotherapeutic approach that I use, not just because of ACT's popularity, or even because of the scientific studies supporting it's effectiveness, but instead, because I live this approach, it has greatly benefitted me and I am hoping it can be of some benefit in your life. I see this as a way of living more than a set of techniques that you can just read about, agree with, and put down. Every experiential thing that I mention will require diligent practice! I would not ask you to do something that I am not willing to do myself (and I am doing these things). Having said that, it is common from an ACT perspective for therapists using this approach to admit a humbling secret. It is not that I am some guru who has it all together and I have not learned techniques so that no matter what life throws at me, I am able to smile and live in a state of bliss. No way! As they say in the ACT community, "While you are on your mountain over there climbing and facing the difficulties, I am not at the top of your mountain or mine. I am climbing on my mountain facing my own challenges or obstacles, but because of training and my perspective over here, I may be able to warn you and coach you through some of the obstacles you face on your mountain." Does this surprise you? I used to think that most everyone else has it made. I remember often thinking, "why is everyone else so happy and always seem to have such good luck?" I also want to emphasize that anything written here, is meant as something to help you with skills, help you accept who you are, and help you move through life toward your goals - and there will NOT be mention of miraculous CURE here. I don't believe my condition will be cured and (despite some obvious limitations in my life), I wouldn't want to be cured - I love being neurodiverse! That being said, if things aren't going so well in the way that I am responding to the world, then I need to do some things differently - that involves commitment.

Change involves Commitment!

Commitment is not a promise but a process of continuing to do healthy actions, even when you don't feel up it. It means moving in a recovery direction and adjusting your course of actions whenever you find yourself going off course.

Ask myself?

How is commitment different than a promise?

What ways am I showing that I am ready to commit to getting better – to recovery?

Healthy "Auto-Pilot"

We are often stuck in unhealthy auto-pilot, dealing with stress, success, boredom, and emotional pain by often resorting to unhealthy behavior patterns.

As part of changing, we want to "train our brain" into a routine of doing healthy action steps, even when faced with adverse circumstances and the obstacle thoughts that usually follow.

We can train ourselves to go into "healthy auto-pilot" mode, and do healthy behaviors, even if they seem foreign, un-natural, or go against our desire to run, escape, fight, or lash out against the world. In other words, our new recovery behaviors may seem un-natural, or even strange simply because we are not used to doing these healthy behavior patterns.

Stay focused on what is important to you – the kind of life that you want to live.

What sort of healthy behaviors do I want to start doing to "train my brain" and start establishing a "healthy auto-pilot" in response to triggers - and to break old routines?

Exercise: Do things Differently...

Example: I used to... - isolate and not talk to anyone

Example: Now I plan on... sharing things with people who are close to me.

Your turn:

I used to...

Now I plan on...
I used to...
Now I plan on...
I used to...
Now I plan on...

Chapter 2 - Who am I?

Without getting into a bunch of philosophizing, would you agree with me that – based on your life experiences, you have a good idea of what you are good at and what you are not so good at. If you are like me, your mind gives you messages about who you are. Wait a minute! I just said your mind gives **you** – *so who is the "you" that is noticing?* It is almost as if we have two minds, right? It is amazing that we can observe our own thoughts. Because of this remarkable ability to almost step outside the chatter in our mind, we sometimes may say things such as "I told my*self*....". So, we have this chatterbox inside our head (the generator of self-talk) that we can "observe" by recognizing it is there. I sometimes feel as if I have three minds!

First, there is that inner self-talk voice that I just mentioned that communicates good things and bad about: who I am, what I have gone through, and what my future will hold for me. Second, there is the part that listens and often believes what it hears – some of the good, and most of the bad of what the chatterbox says: "Why, did I do that... I am a failure...I can never get things right." Third, there is an **observing mind** that can witness all this. Of course, we are talking figuratively, there are probably not really two or three "minds" that science could probably examine and identify. Sometimes, my observing mind is witnessing a battle that is taking place – for example, if I want to eat something bad for me, like a big chocolate brownie. One part of me proclaims, "You shouldn't eat this, you are wanting to lose weight and be healthy right?" Another part of me replies, "Go ahead, you can eat a salad and exercise later." Then, the observing mind witnesses each side present these opposing arguments until an action is taken – I either eat the brownie or I walk away from it.

I have heard that we tend to absorb more negatives than positives. Clinical experience as a therapist, tells me that this is true (and personal experience of telling myself negative things and thinking of examples which support the negatives comes on strong, based on my experiences in this mostly neurotypical world). Several times, I have asked, in a group of clients, for each client to make two separate lists. On one list, I instructed them to "write down everything that you can remember, in your whole life, that people have said to you that was positive, kind, encouraging, and so forth – all positives!" After everyone in the group completed the positive list, I then instructed them, "Now, write a list of everything that you can remember, in your whole life, that people have said to you that was negative, mean, discouraging, and so forth – all negatives!". Guess which list was much longer – even in those clients who self-identified as having good "self-esteem"? You guessed it, the negatives. I was surprised to find that most everyone tended to remember many negatives, even when someone in the past said a negative as a joke or mild tease, it was still remembered well.

I like to think of mindfulness as a practice, not a technique. Mindfulness then becomes a process of cultivating the observing mind. Many people think of mindfulness as being the ability to be aware of your surroundings and being able to take in all the beauty, sounds, and everything happening around you – *outside* of your body. Being able to have that type of awareness is important. I believe it is equally as important to be able to be aware and observe what is happening *inside* of you as well. No, I am not talking about listening to your stomach growl. Being able to listen to that negative and positive chatter in your brain and have the ability to mentally step outside of you inner chatter while being aware of what it is – a collection of thoughts, opinions and observations, is what I feel is extremely important in the practice of mindfulness. However, I also believe that if your goal in practicing mindfulness is to use it as a quick fix technique so that you can "turn off" only the negative chatter, then that would not be true mindfulness. In mindfulness, we hear everything there, but learn when to give our power and attention to and when not to.

WBAD RADIO – Broadcasting criticism 24 hours a day – seven days a week!

Have you ever listened to a radio program that you disagreed with? Maybe you are politically conservative, and the liberal radio station is on and someone is saying something you totally disagree with. Or maybe you are liberal and the conservative station is blaring loud and the talk radio host is saying something that you disagree with. You hear it, you listen, but do you have to believe and agree with what the person with the opposite viewpoint is saying? Of course not! So then, do you have to believe everything that your mind tells you? If there is an important newsflash from your mind, for example, "Look out, that truck is about to hit you!" – that may be important to listen to, as it could save your life. However, will believing "I am worthless and a failure" do much to benefit me? Will it help me live the life I want to live?

Fusion and Defusion – Don't believe everything that you hear, even from *you*!

Exercise: Look at the following list, and see if have you heard any of these? If you haven't heard them, have you somehow received these messages through society?

Big boys don't cry.

Asking for help is a sign of weakness.

If you are not able to do your work (or work at all) then you are lazy!

If it is really important, you *would* remember it!

Maybe you should try *harder* (or work longer hours, etc.)

The more money you make, the more important and worthwhile you are.

Everything happens for a reason – you just need to move on.

Do you ever find yourself saying these types of things to yourself? (see below)

"I should... (be more successful, make more money, have a bigger house, not made bad choices)!"

"I must (do better, have everyone like me, not make mistakes)!"

So what is fusion?

Fusion is when we bond so much to a thought, a rule, our roles, our feelings, our memories or any other product of our mind so much that it seems to be a fact of life to live by.

Have you noticed that at a social event, when someone is introducing himself or herself, how often will people introducing themselves to each other tell each other what their job title is? A career choice is something that many people become fused with: "I am Doctor Smith", "I am a police officer", "I work as a carpenter". If who you are, that is how you think of yourself – your identity, is tied to your job, what happens to your identity when you lose your job, retire, or if you become disabled?

Sometimes, a person will identify with their abilities or talents: "I am a musician, I play the piano", "I am a cross country runner", "I am an artist". Once again, what happens if you lose those abilities that you think make you who "you" - "are"? I have seen many people have an empty identity and go into despair when fusion with a role happens.

It is not that I think a person should not identify whatsoever with a role. However, I don't believe it is healthy if the fusion is so strong that the person cannot move beyond these roles if adversity happens. In my own experience, I personally pride myself with being a Judo martial artist. I worked hard to get a black belt and love the sport of Judo. I sometimes think of myself as being a *good* Judo athlete. However, when I hold very strongly to the "good" part, I may feel like I should win most if not all of my matches. Then, if I lose a match or am not able to do well at Judo on a particular day, I become uncomfortably humbled whenever I lose a match. If much of my identity depended on my being a Judo athlete, and let's say I was disabled in a car accident, then I easily lose my identity. If you have something that you are passionate about, can you hold onto it, but hold it lightly? Do you have the ability to redefine that aspect of yourself, should the time come when you can't do that job, talent, role?

How much unnecessary suffering is brought upon you by following societal expectations or other rules that you have learned to live by? Do you find yourself trying to live up to other's expectations of how you *should* be?

Being neurodiverse, or ND, you might have a low opinion of yourself (or more accurately, a collection of many low opinions about yourself). You may have been frustrated, criticized, made-fun of, viewed with "the look" from NT's of being "less than" others in worth, being shamed, and put down enough that you have a hard time thinking of yourself with many (or any) positive descriptors. Self-acceptance is the recognition that you are a worthwhile human being with faults and strengths – you are okay! Self-acceptance does NOT mean there is no room for improvement or growth.

Let's step back and think about what we have just been talking about: 1) our mind gets fused (hooked, bonded to, over identified) with our thoughts, feelings, roles, rules/expectations, feelings; 2) self-esteem is part of that fusion, when you are fused with the positive or negative opinions of yourself; 3) self-acceptance (in contrast) is allowing yourself to be human and recognize your strengths, recognizing your weaknesses and letting yourself do what you can, in order to improve upon the parts of yourself that you are able.

So, what do we do when we find fusion is causing us increased suffering (we get enough from life as it is, yet sometimes we increase our own suffering)? The opposite of fusion is **defusion** – more on this later.

Exercise: Rewriting your story

Your mind generates stories based on interpretations of your past circumstances, current events, and even predicts the future. Just take the facts and re-write a possible story of your life (including a healthier outcome for the future). The outcome must be psychologically healthy and realistic. The new story is not about replacing negatives with positives or thinking magically, it is just a reinterpretation of the factual circumstances from your past and present, just with a more healthy outcome. It doesn't matter if it doesn't come true, but the outcome must be one that could possibly come true with effort, help, and hope!

Chapter 3 - Values and Goals

People often confuse values with goals. A goal is something that be accomplished and crossed off on a list. A value is something that is worked for and not something you can obtain (or cross off on a list). For example, having a child is a goal, but being the best parent that you can is a value. Both are subjective. Values can be relationships, ideals, etc. Values also consist of what you care about in life - or what you want to stand for, be known for, etc.

Examples of values:

I care about my health

I care about helping other people

I want to be the best parent I can be

I want others to remember me as being kind and caring

Notice that it would be easy to get fused to a value. Values are extremely important for generating life directions or goals, but you probably want to be very careful not to hold values too tightly. I can value my relationship with my wife to the extent that if she divorces me, or gets killed in an accident, I would feel like I was nothing without her. Likewise, if I am fused with my health to the degree that I exercise, eat properly, yet still somehow end up with a heart attack or get diagnosed with a chronic or even terminal illness, I could lose my identity.

Mind-boggling, isn't it? First, I tell you it is important to recognize your values, because these will determine the direction that you want to go for a vital, meaningful life, but then I tell you at the same time to hold on to these lightly! In a pinch, you need to be able to shift, to re-define, to regenerate – in other words it takes learning to be flexible.

It is important to set goals. When setting goals, make sure your goals are values-driven, meaning that they are consistent with and help maintain your values. Goals should be measurable and - ideally, they are both realistic and obtainable (especially immediate goals). Small goals can lead to larger ones (i.e. short term goals vs. long term goals). When setting goals, never set a passive goal. A passive goal is something that a dead person could do better than someone living. Examples of passive goals are items like: "not being depressed", "not having another anxiety attack", "quitting smoking", etc. A dead person doesn't get depressed, nor does he or she have an anxiety attack, etc. In order to change a passive goal to a live goal, ask yourself what you would do instead, in the absence of those things. For example: "If I wasn't depressed, I would get out of the house more and socialize with others." This gives you something to work on, in which you can begin to work on it right away.

Values and Goals

If you have no clue what your goals are, ask yourself how you would want to be remembered after you leave this planet. You could also pretend someone was filming a documentary about your life, as you started changing, think about what the audience might see on the film that was different at the end of the documentary? What would other people notice that you were doing differently? How about six months to a year or two later, if you continued healthy changes, what would you do or accomplish that you otherwise wouldn't have?

So what are some of the things (not literally "things" materialistically) that you care about? In other words, what is important to me?

What do I want to stand for in life?

What gives or could give my life meaning and a sense of purpose?

What activities or goals would help me become the kind of person that I want to be?

Obstacles

What stands in my way of my values or in living a life of vitality and purpose or meaning?

What is it that I am doing (or not doing) that is not working?

What do I have total control over?

What do I have little control over?

What do I have NO control over?

What is the next small step that you *could* do, to move closer to your values?

Core Values Inventory

Which value would you choose (pretend that you had to have the other two fall apart)? [choose only one]:

Happiness OR Health OR Wealth?

Keep in mind: If you choose "happiness" your health will fall apart and you will only live a short time (say one to two weeks, and you would have to use all your money for medical expenses, etc.) If you choose

"Health", you will live a long full life, but be very miserable, unhappy and very poor. If you choose "Wealth", you will have all the money and be able to take care of family and satisfy all your desires but suffer from severe depression and still will not live very long.

Picture yourself living the remainder of your life under the condition of the value that you choose but with the loss of the other values.

What would life be like?

What does this say about what is important to you?

Next, what if you could only choose two of the following?

Happiness OR Health OR Wealth OR Family?

Keep in mind: What is remaining falls apart. Now, how does life look?

What does this say about what is important to you?

Now rank the six most important people, things, or aspects that are most important to you: (i.e. my health, my job, my brother, my health, my house)

Now, looking at this list – if you had to take away item #6, what would life be like (think about this for minute or two)?

Now item #5 is gone too, now what would life be like (reflect on this for a while)?

Now item #4 is also gone, what would life be life?

Now item #3 is gone too, now what is life looking like?

Do the same with item #2, reflecting on the loss and how that would impact your life.

What are you left with?

If you lost item #1, what would happen?

What does this say about what is important to you?

REFLECTION: What is the most important thing that I should focus on? What do I want to stand for in life or have my life be about?

What do I need to focus my appreciation on? Write your thoughts/reflection down on a piece of paper.

Chapter 4 – The ACE Agenda

I have a confession, actually several confessions. I don't like being criticized. I don't like speaking in a large group of people (and sometimes smaller ones). I am not good at eye contact. I don't like to make a mistake, and do not like it when someone points out my mistake in front of others. I often get my words mixed up and get tongue-tied. I tend to twitch, which I don't like. I also randomly say things that don't make sense (some people think I do these things to be funny, I don't). I wish I could not have forgetfulness (and I was tested and told that for whatever reason, I have memory problems). I also don't like suffering, anxiety, feeling like crap, etc.

When faced with things that you don't like, what is your natural inclination? Do you move toward those things or away from them?

It is no wonder that in a western society, we have learned that you shouldn't suffer and that there are plenty of methods for escape. We chase after happiness to avoid pain and we may practice many forms of escape that are all around us. We are bombarded with commercials for things that will make us happy like new cars, bigger value meals, medications, instant–cure products, and all sorts of things that will make us smarter, better looking, have more money, get things faster and so forth. We have drugs, booze, sex, and all sorts of instant gratification items and pain-avoidance routes. What is the long-term gain for these things: dependence on materialism, illness, addiction, and more increased suffering!

The messages we receive: if you have a headache - go take some medication, get rid of it. If you don't like your job, some beers after work will help! And do these things really work in the long run?

I am not preaching to you to give up everything and become a monk or nun. I just would like you to reflect on something. Are you trying to escape or avoid things that, in the long run, when maybe it would be more beneficial if you faced these things?

It may seem strange, but I find that willingness to experience life vs. avoiding the negative aspects will actually help us grow. Sometimes strategies of escape and avoidance can be a good thing - especially when they are healthy (like taking a walk, taking a vacation, etc.). I have noticed that when we distance ourselves from things that we don't want to face, it temporarily takes us away from the tough issues around us, but we have to eventually return to them.

Avoidance, Control and Escape include actions such as fighting off, repressing, drowning, avoiding, and other actions that numb, push away, or resist life. The opposite of escape, control and avoidance, is acceptance, and the next pages talk some about this. I call our attempts to avoid, control, and escape the ACE agenda! It comes natural to us, but often times it leaves us in turmoil when we find out that avoiding sometimes causes us to miss out on life and things that are important to us, control often doesn't work because we can't control everything, and escaping doesn't work because sleeping, drinking/drugging and other ways of escaping often create more problems for ourselves or others!

ACE exercise: On a sheet of paper, write down some of the feelings, thoughts, and experiences that you try to escape or avoid (or spend valuable time trying to control). Write some of your most popular ways you use this dysfunctional ACE agenda. Next to each thing that you list, write down unhealthy actions that you do (include physical actions and even mental actions such as time worrying) that waste valuable moments of your life and cause you more problems in the long run.

Acceptance vs. Tolerance

Typically, I wait until later in the therapy process with my clients to explain the difference between acceptance and tolerance, for a good reason. When a client first enters therapy, he or she typically has a problem *that he or she wants to get rid of.* Any talk about acceptance of the problem, typically is interpreted as "live with it!" In which case, the client would naturally respond, "That is what I have been doing – I have been living with my (OCD, ADD, Asperger's Syndrome, anxiety, depression, addiction....) – and I can't stand living this way!"

A client who hears about the concept of acceptance also hears "hopelessness". The client proclaims, "You mean that this is the way it's going to be – I will never get rid of this and there is no hope for me?" No, acceptance is NOT hopeless resignation and giving into defeat. Acceptance is recognizing and allowing things to be there that are beyond your control. Acceptance doesn't mean that if you are in an abusive relationship or hostile work environment, that you should sit back and allow it, you can still work to get out and/or do what you can, to get in a healthier, safer situation.

I will emphasize a point again; acceptance is not the same thing as tolerance. Tolerance means "living with something, and it still distresses you". Tolerance is probably not a strong enough word. "Hopelessness" is probably a better way to describe this state of mind – "I have tried ***everything*** – therapy, medication, alcohol, self-help books and <u>nothing works</u>!

Acceptance doesn't mean that you have to like something either - and even if the emotions cause you problems or pain, you can find that you are able to sometimes accept the unwanted emotion by *making room for it*, but not allowing it to interfere with accomplishing your ambitions and valued-driven goals. Make room for it, but *don't allow it to be bigger than you.* Again, when control fails, acceptance is something that allows you to move on, knowing that fighting it is not worth your time and energy.

As a person becomes very good at practicing mindfulness, he or she may get to a point where he or she can still feel the full anxiety, pain, etc. but not let it be distressing enough to interfere with his or her life. Again, you may struggle with how this differs from just "ignoring it" or "tolerating it" or "living with it" *but there is a difference*, and only with consistent practice will you be able to see this difference. **The goal is not symptom reduction or cure, which is yet another control technique to avoid or get rid of (or cure), but instead the goal is *psychological flexibility*.** Psychological flexibility is being able to control the one thing that you DO have control over, your responses. Keep in mind that you will not always be successful in defusing from some upsetting thoughts (I promise, we will discuss more about that later), nor will you be successful at always accepting all your unwanted emotions.

"But I refuse to feel this way!" "I need to get rid of my panic attacks, not be depressed anymore..." Okay, if you want to go back to control efforts, do so - *if* you can find one that works and keeps working. Most of the people that I have worked with, have found that control efforts (when applied to aspects of life that are difficult or impossible to control) are either limited or not always successful (and some are destructive or unhealthy, as I already mentioned). We cannot always control what pops into our mind: images, thoughts, memories, and feelings. When we learn that much of what comes into our head in the form of emotions and thoughts is beyond our control, then we can also recognize that we don't have to obey our mind and know that we can view thoughts as they are, just words (images and feelings) in our mind, nothing more or less. The language in our mind is our opinion. If these thoughts are helpful (or at least not harmful), pay attention to them, if not, learn how to observe them and at least not give them as much power. Practicing mindfulness (defusion, acceptance, and awareness) doesn't mean that our problems will go away or that the way we are will be "fixed" (remember we are not defective or broken – we are who we are). However, a "byproduct" of acceptance may be that we feel better. If nothing else, we learn a better way of responding to unwanted emotions than some of the old unhealthy ways. An anxious person who can learn not to be as distressed by anxious thoughts and feelings – finds that these thoughts and feelings decrease over time: as if the anxiety itself has learned it can't win against such a tough foe. However, those who have set the goal of mindfulness as a magic fix to get rid of unwanted emotions, typically say "I tried what you said, and it doesn't work". This is because the client's mindfulness practice was used as another avoidance technique (just as someone may use drugs, alcohol, avoidance, etc).

We must also remind ourselves we are not going to be perfect at anything, even mindfulness and change. In my opinion, self-acceptance is an important concept. Self-Acceptance is accepting your "self" for who you are including past mistakes, weaknesses, strengths, everything. Self-acceptance may entail some level of self-forgiveness. It also encompasses having the ability to sometimes laugh at yourself. Self-acceptance also allows for improvement.

Whenever you do (and you will) get trapped into seeing yourself as your limited self – the "self" that you attribute aspects to AND when you lose an ability (or acquire a limitation, health problem, retire, etc.) – it is important that you find a new way to loosely re-define your "self". What CAN you do? Even if you are limited to a wheelchair, you can still do something that honors your values.

Willingness vs. Wanting

Again, it is very easy to confuse **willingness** and <u>wanting</u> (your desire for something). Take anxiety for example, specifically: either a panic attack or a frustration meltdown. Note: I refer to a meltdown as an emotional breakdown following a stressor, where I experience intense anxiety and may not respond rationally and/or exhibit behaviors that indicate anxiety, anger, isolation, or disassociation. I do NOT want to have either a panic attack or a meltdown. I would much rather not have anxiety *and all that goes with it.* The problem is, when this anxiety surfaces, the more I try to fight it, repress it, or simply not want it, the more weapons it throws at me. If I don't want it, I have it. However, It is truly possible for me to be willing to have the anxiety, without wanting it to be there. In other words, I can welcome it without liking it.

Contrary to what most self-help books, and popular psychology notions of "being happy and staying happy" tell us, it is important to note: when looking at life from a realistic perspective, pain is a *necessary* part of life. You can't have love, relationships, or take risks without experiencing some emotional pain (and in my Judo class, physical pain as well). As stated before, uncomfortable thoughts and emotions *will happen* regardless of whether we desire them to be there. You can sometimes fight these off, but not as often or easily as more than many of all the books and psychologists would like us to believe. That is why I keep emphasizing that when you can't easily control these thoughts (and you have tried and tried) yet, sometimes the healthiest action (or only option that you have left) is, to accept them. It is interesting that many books and guidelines define happiness as being the norm, <u>the standard</u>. According to popular views, if a person is not happy, he or she is defective. However, I have studied, learned and discovered that many people do get depressed, and that suicidal thinking is very common. It is - by no means - desirable to be in a state of lasting unhappiness, <u>but is happiness truly the *norm*</u>? Are we defective if we are not happy most of the time? In regard to mental disorders, it is often not the affliction (depression or anxiety) that keeps us from doing meaningful activities, because it is possible to do actions even when a person feels depressed or anxious. It is the language in our mind that influences us to be stuck. If you are hearing me point the finger of blame in that, I am not. There is no blame – I am not assigning fault. If you mind spouts out negativity, you are only human. You are also not alone in having negative content flash through your mind, most of us ND do! The reality is that not everyone is happy. We also may find ourselves listening to our own mind when it tells us there is nothing we can do about it. There is an old Zen saying that I find wise: "The way out, is through." Are you willing to experience some discomfort in order to be able to better handle discomfort?

An important concept that goes hand and hand with willingness is that of **workability.** Many times, our thoughts tell us we can't do things because we are too anxious, depressed, etc. If we believe that we must wait until we are free from anxiety, depression, etc. to accomplish things, we may be in for a VERY long wait. Workability is accomplishing things, *while* having the uncomfortable thoughts and emotions. This includes daily tasks, short-term goals, life ambitions, and living by our values. I plow through the snow to accomplish what I need to (the snow remains, but I decide that I have to move my feet in the direction of my valued-driven goals – instead of staying stagnant or running the other way). Sometimes, I may need to ask for help to get through the snow. In this example, the snow represents problems in our lives (I sometimes have a hard time with analogies, so I thought a little bit of explanation may help some of you). This doesn't have to mean, "Grin and bear it!" though. I know, this is easier said than done, and as I said before, you will sometimes get caught up in the thoughts and emotions, we all do. Remember though, avoidance often leads to more pain.

Another example: if I had depression and I didn't feel like getting out of bed, socializing, working, or doing anything fun, it may seem like the thing to do would be to remain in bed - after all, I don't *feel* like getting out of bed. However, the very avoidance strategy of remaining in bed further *increases* my depression – because: I am not doing anything for my health, not gaining interaction with others (and all the while, being fully aware that I am not doing anything of significance). A vicious cycle is then set up.

Mental events: spam of the mind

If you are part of the computer age and you have been using a computer, you are probably familiar with email. Some email is factual, truthful and important. Some of our email gets filtered out into what we call spam or junk mail. Then, there are emails that look and sound important and believable, but they are not. These unproductive emails are mixed in with the upcoming important events or news and may seem "real".

Something (such as a spam email) is often more believable if it is has a picture or video attached to it, but also more dangerous if it is not real, or if it is not good for our computer, but we may buy into it.

Our mind is like a computer, and it is a producer of mental events that may be similar to email. We often call them "thoughts". Some of these mental events contain pictures, mental videos and evoke emotion in us. Sometimes we just have the emotion "sent" to us without a particular thought to go with it. Often the videos contain memories of some past event, or perhaps our angle of interpretation on a current happening, or a prediction video about our future.

If you are like most humans on this planet, you probably have joined the club of seeing your thoughts as being: A) who "you" are, and B) being "true", or at least believable - and you probably (like most of us) often have difficulty determining what is "spam" of the brain and what isn't.

Many therapies encourage us to get good at identifying this mental "spam" and refuting it, meaning we just target certain things as not believable or relevant, which is difficult to do.

Wouldn't it be good if we could – first and foremost, be able to separate and see it ALL (not just filtering out the negative thoughts) as email (all thoughts = just mental products), and that many of these thoughts are not something we have to attach much importance to? If we examined these mental products to weigh out whether they were workable at helping us live a better life or not, we may not be as fused or married to our unworkable mental events (the real, the true, the scary, all of it). This doesn't mean we have to be a detached zombie; we can still laugh and cry and feel what comes to us. But now, we may have the time to leave the "computer" when we need to, and then tend to things that really matter.

Are you following me or lost? If you are lost, I hope the next chapter will provide further elaboration as we are going to revisit the idea of fusion and discuss defusion. This aspect of mindfulness will help us better handle some of the thoughts that we have that lead us away from vitality.

What problems have been caused in your life, created from your paying too much attention to certain thoughts and giving them power?

Chapter 5 – Thought Distancing

Recognizing our workable (Constructive) VS. unworkable (Obstacle) thinking

Point 1: We get "hooked" on our thoughts

We usually view our thoughts as being 100% accurate. In other words, we "buy in" to our thoughts – something called cognitive fusion, which means that we are unable to separate ourselves (and objective reality) from our thoughts. Ultimately, it is not as important whether the thought is actually true, but more importantly:

If you believe it (because you can believe thoughts that are not necessarily true), or

If the thought is helpful, or what I call workable or constructive thoughts (healthy, productive, etc.) in allowing you to accomplish your ambitions (what I call your "dream house") or motivates you to take healthy action steps.

Constructive thoughts and healthy action steps lead you toward a meaningful life. Obstacle and destructive thoughts and actions are ones that you pay attention to or obey, but they lead you away from your values and the meaningful, vital life. If you find yourself buying in to many obstacle or self-destructive thoughts, practice reminding yourself that these are just thoughts - nothing more than mind chatter. Your brain is a good chatterbox.

As previously mentioned, we often take our thoughts at face value, as being facts about what the world around us is like, what we must do, etc. Once again, thoughts are the *language of the mind*. When you have a problem in the external world (i.e. a very vicious dog is outside of your front door, and you need to go out and get your mail), the thinking mind that you have, was designed to problem solve, and might come up with possible solutions – ***I must get rid of this!*** (OR) **I must avoid it** ("I could call Animal Patrol, I could throw a newspaper at it or yell at it to go away", "I'll just stay inside until it goes away and do something else, etc.). It is only logical then that you would naturally try to use this same survival mechanism of problem solving applied to your inner self, such as when you have unwanted emotions, the thinking mind kicks in and does what it was designed to do, to problem solve "I must get rid of this feeling (or avoid it)" – just as it would do with an external problem. These attempts at controlling our thoughts and emotions that I have called forms of avoidance and escape in one of the previous chapters may also be referred to as "control and avoidance strategies". It can become a full-time job to try to get rid of uncomfortable emotions. The cost in control and avoidance strategies is that they use up much time and energy. The time and energy that is spent to deal with unwanted emotions (or what we may want to call mental disorders at their extreme) may result in the avoidance of daily life tasks or meaningful activities. Based on what you have read so far, I hope you can see that when time and energy is spent in unhealthy control and avoidance strategies, relationships are damaged, your health is jeopardized, or you may wind up with something else to get upset about (getting a DUI or possession charge, verbally bashing someone you love, hurting yourself, etc.) Being stuck in our own mind means not living the valued-driven lifestyle that we want to.

Therefore, getting hooked on thoughts means that we are unable to separate ourselves (and often objective reality) from our thoughts. I find that it is not as important whether the thought is actually true but more important: 1) whether you believe it (because you *can* believe thoughts that aren't true), or 2) whether the thought is helpful (healthy, productive, etc.) in allowing you to accomplish your ambitions (what I call values-driven goals) and accomplish the daily tasks which can help your health (mental and physical).

Point 2: We can practice "cognitive defusion": *one part of the practice of mindfulness*

Many people who have heard of the term "mindfulness" may associate it with eastern philosophy or some new age movement. However, in the context of recent research studies, mindfulness is something that doesn't have to involve meditation or have to have any religious tone. In this context, the goal is not enlightenment. Mindfulness is also something that would need to be practiced frequently (daily if possible) in order to cultivate it. It is not something that one can read about and then just immediately know it. Just as if I told you how to do a certain Judo throw, unless you practice it and experience it, just hearing about how to do it will not teach you how to throw it.

There are many techniques a person can use to develop defusion that come from founders and practitioners of Acceptance and Commitment Therapy (ACT). I describe below, some of my favorite techniques. Another way of thinking about this aspect of mindfulness, of distancing yourself from thoughts (cognitive defusion), is in being able to step back from your thinking self and observing it – just as a curious scientist would (remember all of the talk I did about the observing mind earlier?). In this sense, you can see thoughts for what they are, just thoughts. It is not about eliminating a particular thought but instead to distance *you* from it.

In summary, cognitive **de**fusion is the practice of being able to ***not*** get hooked by *all* your thoughts, particularly many of the ones that are unhelpful to you progressing (living a meaningful life despite your limitations and the obstacles in front of you).

Be Mindful! – We CAN learn to not pay as much attention to this negative "thought factory" that we call our "mind" ...

Mindfulness: the practice of paying attention to, but not "buying in" to the obstacle thoughts that your mind will throw at you – nor the self-destructive thoughts that lead you downhill!

Some obstacle thoughts lead to unworkable behaviors if you pay too much attention to these. These obstacle and self-destructive thoughts stand in our way like big bully kids on a playground. Some of these common obstacle thoughts may include:

* I am going to fail sometime, might as well be now!

* There is no hope for me!

* I am under way too much stress. I can't handle it anymore!

* I just don't care what happens anymore!

* Just a little bit, to take the edge off!

* I'll just do this tonight and then get back on track tomorrow.

* Things will never get better, just one darn thing after another!

* I am just too depressed to do anything, can't motivate myself.

I am just a burden to others.

What specific thoughts have you been paying too much attention to lately, and that are leading you nowhere productive?

Another Metaphor for looking at our thoughts & feelings: Thoughts as Bullies

Difficult thoughts, feelings, memories, and sensations "bully" you! They fool you into trying to pay your attention to them so that they can guide your from your path.

How are your thoughts and feelings like bullies?

Some mindfulness techniques*:

"My mind is telling me..." - one way to do some mindfulness and distancing from thoughts is to preface some thoughts (particularly ones that are unhelpful) with the statement: "My mind is telling me"

Examples: "My mind is telling me that I can't tolerate any more anxiety". "My mind is telling me that I am anxious and having the thought that I can't control myself." "My mind is telling me that I was stupid for doing that.". You can also do "My mind is giving me the feeling of..."

Knowing your stories - When I make a mistake or embarrass myself, I may feel inadequate or incompetent and criticize myself "I am sure dumb and incompetent". I can then recognize that my mind is throwing a familiar story at me: "Okay mind, here comes the same old I am dumb, *I am a failure story*, and I don't care about getting pulled into it, no thank you." This can be applied in many situations: "Here comes the old *I am going to screw up my sobriety at some point anyway, so I might as well drink now, story*".

Treat your mind as a separate person - "Thank you mind for that thought, but it wasn't helpful." or label the disorder part of your mind: "Thanks (OCD, addiction, depression, anxiety, ADHD, Asperger's, or simply just 'mind') for those thoughts, but I have stuff that I need to do without you getting in the way".

Put your thoughts outside of yourself - watch your thoughts fly by imagining they are messages on a cloud, or billboards on passing busses. Writing down your thoughts also allows you to put them outside yourself, so that you can see them as being words. You could also imagine your thoughts coming out of your armpit or foot to further lessen their power. Pretend your thoughts or urges are passengers on a bus, demanding that you break from your destination, trying to bully you and convince you to head in the wrong direction. As you continue driving the bus, you keep picking up passengers "Guilt", "Bad Memory", "Incompetent", etc.

Changing the movie or soundtrack - Repeat disturbing thoughts using a comical voiceover. For disturbing images: picture the disturbing image being displayed or played on a TV screen far across the room, (also you can add a musical soundtrack or imagine badly dubbed voiceovers) to lessen the horror of the image. This can also work for situations when you have a catastrophic image of something bad happening in the future.

Critical Radio – this was mentioned earlier: try treating the flow of critical, negative or intrusive thoughts that come from your mind as being like a radio station – you can hear it blasting WBAD, broadcasting bull-crap 24 hours a day, seven days a week - "All criticism and analyzing – all the time". Even though you can't turn the radio off, you can choose to go about accomplishing things without paying attention to the stream of biased talk-radio it produces.

*For more ideas: purchase the book: *The Happiness Trap,* by Russ Harris, MD; *Get Out of Your Mind and Into Your Life,* by Steven C. Hayes, PhD; or *Things Might Go Terribly, Horribly Wrong,* by Kelly G. Wilson, PhD. There are also other books that use Acceptance and Commitment Therapy that are out or in the works.

Remember, in order to develop that observing part of yourself, you must practice frequently. You will still sometimes get suckered into being entangled in some thoughts, as you are only human, but this practice can often help you separate from thoughts at points of time *when you need to,* and then allow you to have more opportunities to not allow thoughts to keep you stuck.

Why not just replace negative (irrational or dysfunctional thoughts) with positive ones?

Picture this scenario: You are a therapist who practices traditional cognitive behavioral therapy (replacing irrational thoughts or cognitive distortions with alternative thoughts). You happen to be the therapist for a young woman, who - during the process of therapy, identifies that she has terrible social skills and has doubts about her intellectual abilities. She states that she would get higher grades in a college class if she participated by answering some of the professor's questions. The young lady tells you that she is afraid to speak up in class. Not only is she afraid to speak in class, she also tells you that she would like to socialize more and make friends, especially some that attend that class. She doesn't want people to laugh at her for saying something "stupid". Furthermore, she has observed that there is a young man in the class that she has an interest in and also, wishes that he would be interested enough in her to date her, but she believes herself to be too unattractive.

As a traditional cognitive behavioral therapist, you assist her with identifying her "irrational" thoughts, her "cognitive distortions": and determined that the following two self-defeating thoughts that she has, stand out: "I am not very intelligent and if I speak up in class, I will be made fun of," and "I am unattractive and an attractive young man in my class would have no interest in me or be repulsed". Next, you assign her to look for evidence of these beliefs in her life, so she points out times in her life when she felt dumb and unattractive. As her therapist, you challenge her that her thoughts are dysfunctional and label these as "cognitive distortions" and encourage her to speak up in class, that she is not likely to be made fun of. You also challenge her to approach the young man, as you believe that he may find her attractive, and emphasize to her that it is only her belief that she is not. So, she speaks up in class, and answers one of the professor's questions with what she believes to be a very good answer. Unfortunately, her answer is so ludicrous to those around her that the entire class starts laughing. She runs out of the class crying, more convinced of her stupidity. Later, in the dining area of her college, she sees the young man at lunch. She takes your second piece of advice and approaches him about possibly dating her. The young man rudely answers her, "if you had plastic surgery and got rid of that ugly nose and lost some weight, I may consider dating you if you were the last person on the planet". She now feels even worse and withdraws from society more. Lesson learned: we can replace one thought with another, but the replacement thought is still a thought. It is still an attempt at control. In this hypothetical example, you, as the therapist, had your own thoughts: a) that the woman was probably intelligent and b) in your opinion, you personally had not seen anything wrong with her appearance. Whether or not you were actually right or wrong about her actual intelligence or appearance, neither of your thoughts (nor advice) was workable at helping her become more social or change her beliefs, and now the negative beliefs that she had about herself were further reinforced. When we attempt thought replacement, the "new thought(s)" may not lead us closer toward our goals than the "irrational" thoughts that are replaced. Once again, thoughts are thoughts. Remember: when weighing out the extent to which you are "married" or fused to a particular thought, it may be more beneficial in helping you decide whether to detach from it based on it's workability: will this thought enhance my life by bringing me closer to my goals, and benefit myself as well as those whom I care about? OR Is this thought not very workable towards leading me to my goals, causes destruction in my life or in the lives of those whom I care about?

In the role of a therapist, instead of looking toward a positive alternative reality, I may have her explore her values. If speaking up and taking the risk of people laughing at her are worth it to her - in order to possibly achieve a better grade, or possibly be able to either get a date OR handle social rejection feelings. If the risks associated with speaking in class are worthy of taking, in order to move in the direction of her valued-driven goals, she may decide to go through with it, while knowing that the outcome <u>may not be positive.</u>

Are you starting to get the hang of these two aspects of mindfulness? Cultivate the observing part of your mind to see your thoughts as if from an outside witness perspective. Look at the thoughts, rules, roles, and expectations that you are fused with. Allow the thoughts to be there, practice watching the thoughts pass by, pretend they are on clouds or leaves. Thank your mind for a thought, but don't allow it to dominate you – just as you might thank a pesky kid or obnoxious teenager that gives you his opinion on your clothing, but remembering it is just a bunch of biased opinion.

Pay attention to the thoughts that will move you toward a vital meaningful life. Know your stories - "here comes the 'I am a failure' story", "here is the 'poor me' story", etc.

Using observation and awareness we can pull back the mental filter we have that we see the world through.

The way that I teach mindfulness involves learning what I have called **The Four L's:**

1) **Look**: having awareness and being able to observe as if from a witness/outside observer perceptive.

2) **Listen**: what are the thoughts that you are having? What is your mind telling you?

3) **Label**: being able to see and label thoughts and thoughts, feelings as feelings, etc.

4) **Let it be**: which is not getting rid of, but being able to not give these mental events ultimate power over you (also known as not "buying in" to our thoughts and not becoming "fused" with them).

The four "L"'s in action – some examples:

* **Look**: My boss criticized my project.

* **Listen**: "My mind is telling me (I'm worthless, things are horrible, I can't handle this)"

* **Label**: "I'm (depressing, craving, getting anxious, feeling manic, isolating,)"

* **Let it be**: "It's a thought. It is my depression talking. I don't have to act on it. There my mind goes again. Thank you mind for that thought but.."

Combine the process of mindfulness with doing healthy behaviors despite your unhealthy thoughts. In the next chapter, we will discuss feelings and a possibility for how to handle them.

Practice the four "L"s with thoughts you listed previously and practice these "live" as unhelpful thoughts occur!

Chapter 6 – Feelings and Urges

I have heard many therapists say, "Our thoughts *cause* our feelings!" I had taken this at face value for many years. I tried numerous attempts at the control agenda of trying to change my thoughts and blaming myself for feeling bad because of not doing some thought replacement.

Feelings are influenced by many factors: situational, physical/hormonal, thoughts, and probably many other factors that I have little to no control over. "Wait a minute!", you say, "Didn't you kind of point out earlier that giving our thoughts power makes us feel bad?" Your mind continues, "You also talked about how escape and avoidance strategies cause us to feel bad too! You are contradicting yourself!" Let me be clear: what we do influences our feelings. How we think influences our feelings. How we act, influences our feelings (and we do invite unnecessary suffering by doing destructive or avoidance behaviors). Yes, AND sometimes we just plain feel sad, anxious, crappy, you name it – *just because*. We are human. In addition to not having control over some of the thoughts that pop into our head, we also sometimes don't have control over the feelings that pop into our head. Remember earlier when I talked about panic attacks and meltdowns? Remember when I said that trying to eliminate or control anxiety and emotional meltdowns may actually make them worse?

Expansion

When a feeling comes, I can give it a name: "anxiety". I can give it a shape. I can give it a color. I allow it to be a certain size within me (but not bigger than me). I observe it. I feel it. I know it is there. I allow it to come and stay as long as IT (the anxiety, anger, or whatever feeling it is) wants to. I don't like it, I don't want it, but that is beside the point, it is there inside me. I am willing to have it. I allow it. I know that this particular feeling can't be fought, pushed under a rug. The unwanted feeling is like an uninvited guest, in which case I know that offending this particular unwanted visitor will only provoke the uninvited emotion to get louder and stronger.

Are you willing to have this feeling?

Once again, practice is key. Next time you are frustrated, upset, anxious – whatever you feel, practice observing, allowing and giving it a shape, size and color. Just like thoughts, it is a mental product. You do not have to act destructively on it. You need not punched walls, they are not at fault.

If you would like, draw the feeling on a piece of paper.

Dealing with destructive urges

I used to have meltdowns when I was angry of frustrated as a child (and teenager). I still have urges but (knock on wood) have not done any damage to furniture or people's faces (not counting incidental pain inflicted in Judo classes). My poor mother! When she was living, as a youngster I put her through much with my tantrums and meltdowns, but I was "paid back" by my first-born son, who was ten times more explosive than I ever was!

I also know what it is like to deal with urges, particularly addictive ones. I went through a drink alcohol excessively phase while in college. This phase of heavy drinking ended after I met the woman who would become my wife. I knew my chances of keeping the one close relationship that I had left in life would be destroyed if I didn't change this escape, avoidance and control agenda of drinking that I held onto at that time.

When faced with an urge that is destructive, practice not acting on it. Remember that it is possible to have an urge and ride it out (like a wave until it dissipates). It is important not to act on urges that could harm yourself or someone else (violence, drug/alcohol usage, destroying things, etc.) It may be very hard not to act on something when you are experiencing heavy urges. Just remember, there is no rule that says that you must absolutely act on the urge - no matter what your mind tells you!

On a piece of paper, write some of your destructive urges (when your mind pushes you to avoid, repress, do something dangerous, drink/do drugs, etc.):

The Obstacles (barriers to growth)
Obstacle Thoughts

What memories, worries, fears, self-criticisms, or other unhelpful thoughts does your mind throw at you that you dwell on, or get "caught up" in, related to this issue? What thoughts do you buy into that hold you back, bully you around, or generally bring you down?

Self-defeating Actions/Poor Ways to Cope/Unworkable Behaviors:

What are you currently doing that makes your life worse in the long term: keeps you stuck; wastes your time or money; drains your energy; restricts your life, impacts negatively on your health, work or relationships; maintains or worsens the problems you are dealing with?

Obstacle Feelings

What emotions, feelings, urges, impulses, or sensations (associated with this issue) do you fight with, avoid, suppress, and make attempts to get rid of, or otherwise struggle with?

Obstacles Situations

What situations, activities, people or places are you avoiding or staying away from? What have you quit, withdrawn from, dropped out of? What do you keep "putting off" until later?

Meltdowns

Whether adult or child, people on the spectrum are often known to have episodes of intense anxiety or anger, where they may shut down, or go to the other extreme and act irrational.

Meltdowns are typically the result of:

1) Anxiety Provoking Situations – novel situations, overload of stimuli (bright lights, loud noises, multiple people talking, too many tasks to get done, information overload, tests/exams, performing, public speaking, being put in the spotlight, crowded places, etc.).

2) Frustration – being criticized, underperforming, not achieving a goal or task as desired, limitations that prevent accomplishing something, mistakes, failed efforts.

3) Expectation – when the outcome is different than what was expected and sometimes, what was desired. Not getting the desired object (or person), not being allowed to go somewhere, an unexpected change in schedule, an obstacle or barrier that prevents the desired or expected outcome.

As part of mindfulness and the practice of not acting on destructive urges, we can learn to handle our anxiety, deal in a healthy manner with frustration, and learn to accept that life will not always provide the outcome that we expect. Our next step will be to deal with that outcome in the healthiest way possible.

Recognize your stories:
Your thoughts and feelings combine to form your interpretation of life around you. This combination of interpretations is called "stories", usually they have themes and come up frequently when triggered. Typically, these are variations of a common story theme of being "not good enough".

Your mind, or "inner critic" throws these at you and these common stories bring you down.

* "I am a fraud/my life is a life" (my opinion doesn't matter, I am really not that good, I suck at this, I am not a good _____, I am faking normal, but am a mess on the inside, etc.)

* "My life totally sucks" (nothing good ever happens, life keeps crapping on me, I can't deal with this, it's just one bad thing after another).

* "I am broken" (I can't stand myself, I am a failure, I have screwed everything up, I can't do things like I used to, I have illnesses that I can't do anything to fix, I can't keep up , I don't like who or what I have become).

What are some of your common stories (or themes that are common in your obstacle thoughts)?:

Chapter 7 - Beyond our control

Have you heard of the serenity prayer/poem?

"(God,) Grant me the serenity, to accept the things that I cannot change, the courage to change the things that I can, and the wisdom to know the difference..." - Reinhold Niebuhr

Typically, when you hear "accept the things that I cannot change", what may come to your mind for the "things" is usually life situations and adverse circumstances. We have already explored that there is more than just the things outside of us that we have little to no control - we also can't always stop the thoughts and urges that pop into our heads. As mentioned before these things that pop into our heads may include mental pictures or "videos" of a catastrophic future ahead of us or of past traumas, mistakes, and so on.

Now, we need to go ahead and add to the list of things we can NOT change (thoughts and feelings are things we already mentioned) to include *unwanted life circumstances*. Sometimes it seems that the universe can hand you a pile of doggy poop.

I have commonly heard people proclaim to a counselor or therapist: "You would be depressed too if your son just overdosed on drugs!", "How can I feel good, my wife just left me for another man!", "I just lost my job because my boss is unwilling to work with me and accommodate my issues!" In my field, it is a common mistake of new therapists to try to rush into a fancy technique to try to "get rid of" the client's suffering or feel responsible to attempt to make the client feel better. Truthfully, when you have adverse circumstances happen, you feel bad – because (once again) you are human! I have deep compassion for people in bad circumstances because I have endured death and horrors of my own. Don't get me wrong, I have not experienced everything bad there is to experience, and I can't pretend to know what certain tragedies feel like to a person – this is why I have deep compassion, and I encourage anyone working with others in a helping profession to put that level of compassion first and foremost. By the way, as part of my neurodiverse way of being, I have struggled with empathy. In the place of empathy, I have learned sympathy and compassion. I probably couldn't do great justice in explaining the difference, but to me, sympathy and compassion are when I am able to picture how I would feel if the things the client is reporting to me, happened to me. Empathy is probably a more automatic thing that happens easily for NT's.

It is no wonder that we feel the need to rush through or attempt an avoidance or control and escape agenda when we are in rough circumstances. Society even provides messages (some in policies, some unspoken) that we: shouldn't have meltdowns while at work, should only get three days off of work to grieve if a family members death, and we should "get over it", no matter how severe the "it" that we are suffering from is.

I also feel for the young adults today. Many of today's young adults are in a battlefield and are surrounded by coping mechanisms of illicit drugs, booze and other forms of things to get addicted to.

When adversity hits us (and it will), we can do what we can – that's really all that we can do (I know I am a little tangential). What we are left with after we have exhausted doing all we can, is acceptance. Remember, I can't emphasize enough, acceptance doesn't mean to "grin and bear it", it means we do what we can, given the situation that we are facing. The challenge then, is to move towards the things we care about, despite the cloud of adversity darkening the world around us and making it hard to see the things that we do care about.

"What if I don't have anything to care about?" This is a question often posed to me from someone who has no family, no friends, no pets,

etc. Then, my best advice would be to find something that gives you meaning and purpose. Something that is beneficial to you and possibly to others. Notice I didn't say something that makes you *happy* – then we get back into the game of chasing happiness and the control and avoidance agenda.

Not all of us can walk around expecting good things to happen. I have met people who seem eternally optimistic, and I am envious. Yet, I don't think it is healthy to always be vigilant either (and I have a hard time with this). It is true that you never know when the cosmic 2x4 will hit, but don't walk around looking for it or you will miss out on some of the good things in life happening right in front of you.

The clients that I worked with are often not strangers to loneliness. Even those clients that I was a therapist for who happened to be in the workforce and surrounded by others at work, would often feel lonely. Many of my former clients who have relationships, spouses, support groups, and loving families, STILL felt lonely. When loss occurs (job, relationship, deaths, etc.) it just adds to that despair. If you hear my words of fusion earlier (with job, family, spouse, etc.), you may begin to wonder if the way out of pain is detachment from all those things, but detachment is the same thing as avoidance. Trying to control your feelings of despair is a control strategy. Remember, these avoidance, control and escape strategies do NOT work well in the long run. I have learned that experiencing pain and suffering is a part of life. Defusion helps us continue on with some sense of identity. Again, mindfulness and the defusion techniques involved, are not to detach from life nor are they to keep us from experiencing pain altogether. We practice mindfulness to have flexibility when life presents something difficult to deal with.

It is often helpful when faced with a life crisis to write out the following questions: What can I change (control, have power over, etc.)? What about this can I NOT control, and what do I need to accept? What healthy actions can I take despite this adversity?

The Cosmic 2x4

At any time in our lives, it can strike! It will strike! We never know when it will hit. Things can be "smooth sailing" for a while and then.... POW! Avoiding it is not an option. Escaping from it and numbing from it only prolongs the pain that it brings.

What do we want to do, know, or be aware of before it hits us (and it will strike)?

What do we want to do, know, or be aware of after it hits us?

Without writing it here (personally reflect), what was one time in your life when the Cosmic 2x4 hit, and you didn't handle it well (and still have some things to deal with about this incident)?

Remember: pain is a part of living. No matter how much we want a life without suffering, life finds a way to send us that suffering like a crack under a door or window that allows the cold air to come in. In this house of life, you can try to cover all the cracks and entrances, but the cold air of adversity will still find a way in, and you are ignoring the things that really matter by clinging to these control, escape and avoidance strategies. The reality that "pain is a part of living" is not the same thing as "just live with it" – instead it allows us to recognize that we can't change some unfortunate things, we can also work not to add unnecessary suffering on top of what life dishes out to us.

Serenity Exercise:

What are some things that I can NOT change and must accept (or not try to control, avoid, or escape from)? Note: Not only can these include some life circumstances, but also the obstacle thoughts and feelings that we often can't stop from popping into our heads.

Am I willing and ready to accept myself, including my limitations, the things that I have done that I wished I hadn't and to forgive myself and start taking care of myself?

A Creative Sense of Hopelessness

Have I done everything that I can do, to possibly change to better function in the school, workplace, or as part of a relationship? Do I want to change? Most of us neurodiverse people have asked this question to ourselves numerous times. The answers that we give to ourselves in answering these questions usually either contain elements of self-blame or blaming others (or a combination of both).

Our ways to change in order to function in the school environment, workplace settings, or relationships usually involve one or more of the following:

Assimilation: I learn techniques through observation of others or by learning skills to help better "fit in". This involves the use of planning or organization systems (calendars, software, personal planners, coaches, etc.). I may even try to study or observe body language in an effort to be able to read other people. There are numerous skills and techniques to learn in order to try to accomplish assimilation. To live and function well in today's neurotypical world requires some degree of assimilation on our part.

Accommodations: I ask for help and assistance – either from other people, or obtain assistive devises (just as in assimilation, but beyond what a typical schoolmate, coworker, or person in my circumstance would have as part of an ordinary day). This includes things like: increased time allotted to finish a test at school or work project, any number of assistive devices, a change in job functioning, tutoring in school, being assigned a special education or learning disabled guidance instructors (in school or college), an office away from distraction, etc.

Functional Matching: I find a school or career where my strengths are utilized, and weaknesses are not as evident. I may attend a school where there are others like myself. I may find a career that matches my personality and thinking style (i.e., in my case a job where you don't have to clock in at a certain time or have to memorize math, dates, etc.). I may choose to be involved in a relationship with someone like myself, or with someone who either understands those like me or is a compliment to my thinking style.

What ways can I apply assimilation, accommodations, or functional matching to make my situation better?

Chapter 8 – Putting it together!

A cceptance of my way of being

Having tried numerous times to assimilate, obtain whatever accommodations that I feel comfortable asking for (or that legitimately can be provided), and I have tried to match myself to a school, workplace, or relationship that brings out my best, *suppose I still have great difficulty?* This is the basic reason that I didn't focus on this workbook being entirely about skills. I have read many books on organizational, memory, and communication skills and have found some of these skills helpful to put into practice. Yet, despite all the books on skills that I have read, those times when I have been told things such as "just write everything down" or "ask people to repeat everything to you or speak slowly", it has felt very demeaning. Personally, I have had other professionals give me advice on assimilation and accommodation, but that advice typically only goes me so far in helping me on a day-to-day basis.

Recognizing the limits of what I can accomplish by therapists, medications, coaches, books, planners, assistive devices and so on, there comes a point where I have to face this: if I am doing what I can, and still things are not all well in my functioning, what left is there? This is where the acceptance piece that we talked about earlier comes in. If you skipped that part, please go back and read it, as what I am talking about now will be grossly misinterpreted without an understanding of what acceptance is and isn't.

I must admit that in my professional career, I have been back and forth so much on the advantages and disadvantages of diagnostic labels.

Ultimately, I have concluded (not surprisingly as it is very ACT-like) that, if a diagnosis helps you not blame yourself, or feel not alone, and the label empowers you to make changes in order to get closer to the meaningful life that you want to live, then it is probably worth accepting.

The diagnostic labels that were given to me, I do accept, but instead of naming each one, I like to put them under the broader and not so professional term of "neurodiverse". Sometimes I quietly think of myself as an "Aspie" as it is a label that has a fitting uniqueness to it. If you would rather say you *have (whatever diagnosis' you have been given - such as: Asperger's, ADHD, dyslexia, or whatever)*, please feel free to do so. However, for those of you that have Asperger's, either by the time that you read this, or not too much longer afterward, the term Asperger's may be dropped and replaced as being equivalent to higher functioning autism (or Autistic Spectrum Disorder).

It is personally difficulty for me to always accept the way that I am, and quite frankly difficult for other's around me sometimes. Why? The NT's around me may not see me as being different because (like many others in my situation), *I look perfectly normal.* When I *look* so normal, my behaviors are not as easily forgivable, excusable, or easy for others to stand. This makes self-blame easy and asking for accommodations difficult.

I hate to repeat myself (I do it anyway), but going back to the ideas contained in the serenity prayer: I am working on accepting the things that I can NOT change, having the courage to change what I can, and trying to gain the wisdom to figure out what is what (and that is sometimes difficult). I challenge you to do the same. Get whatever coaching, books, etc. that you can on assimilation. If you are in a position to ask for accommodations (at work or school), and that will not create more problems for you, please do so. If you have done all that you believe you can, learn to accept the parts of yourself that are unique.

Awareness

If I can gain a basic understanding of other people's body language, it can be helpful to observe smiles, frowns, and tone of voice. If I pay too much attention to the content of what someone who is speaking to me is saying, I may miss out on the other nonverbal communication, which may be more important. Awareness of another person's nonverbal communication and hidden meaning behind the verbal words spoken is something that must be practiced and still may not be mastered if you have a similar way of functioning as I do.

Awareness itself is a skill that must be practiced. Next time you are walking outdoors, see if – instead of getting lost in your thoughts – you can notice things around you. Look at the ground, look at leaves on trees. What color is the sky? How does the sun (or lack thereof) feel on my skin?

When you are practicing moment-to-moment or here-&-now awareness, if I thought, feeling or sensation interrupts you, label it and go back into observation mode. For example, I am fully aware and observing a beautiful day. As I walk, I start thinking "I wonder if I will get in trouble for being five minutes late?" Label that thought, "WORRYING", then go back into observing the beautiful day (but walk faster because you are late). See how hard awareness practice can be?

You can even answer or respond to other people from an awareness perspective (particularly when that other person is angry or upset with you). Answering with responses such as the following come from an awareness perspective:

"It sounds to me like you are very frustrated with my tardiness again."

"I feel very upset when I am scolded like this."

"I am thinking that I should make a plan to address this issue and quite honestly feel that I am doing the best that I can."

"I am feeling very upset because it wasn't my intention to upset you."

When answering from an awareness perspective, I can take ownership of my own thoughts and feelings. Keep in mind that when you are communicating from an awareness perspective, it still does not mean that the other person's opinions, anger level, or actions will change.

Steps to Effective Communication - Especially During Conflict

Key Points (these can be combined – they are points not steps that you must follow in order):

1. **Non-Resistance/Non-defensive stance**: find some truth (even the slightest bit) in what the other person is saying. Try not to absorb the negative energy as their goal may be to "throw you off balance" and then you may become defensive. When you become defensive, you may validate negative thoughts that the other person has about you. You also allow yourself to be defeated by unproductive and unhealthy emotions such as anger, hostility, self-pity, and large amounts of anxiety. Also try not to absorb what they are saying. Soaking up negative energy like a sponge is unhealthy. Redirect focus to the problem or that person's perspective (opinion, way of looking at it, life experience, etc.) not to the other person's being (i.e. Attack the issue not the person). We like to call this step "mental Judo".

2. **Ask Questions to clarify and gain perspective**: Acknowledge how the other person is possibly feeling. The attempt is to walk in that person's shoes. Ask questions vs. assuming. Combine questions with paraphrasing the other person's feelings and see if you can understand his or her point of view and to show him or her that you understand. Also, weigh things out from a larger perspective. It is more important that you allow this person to feel what they are feeling and acknowledge that than it is to try to change the person's feeling. Also, before you part-ways or have a falling out, ask yourself "Is this more important than my relationship with this person (do I want to ruin a relationship based on this one thing – does it really matter that much?). If your brain can not process the information clearly, have the person write down his or her arguments, feelings, concerns so that you can take your time and address these later (see #4 below).

3. **Communicate with "I feel statements"**: When you communicate your thoughts and feelings, try to start with a feeling and use an "I feel" format. This lessens the chance of the other person feeling defense (as when you use "you" statements). General statements of accusation and finding fault - such as "you always..., you never...., you need to...." - tend to put people on the defense and closes down productive communication. If it is possible, avoid seeking to prove the person wrong (and yourself right) or engage of the game of winning to gain victory by putting the person down. Another reason for communicating with feeling statements is that it allows the other person the possibility of seeing your perspective and it is hard to argue with a feeling (i.e. "I feel upset when this happens. I feel sad when you do this behavior." – the person would then have difficulty saying "no, you don't feel sad".

4. **A Personal "Time-out" - for Reflection**: Allow yourself time to cool down. By taking time to think things over, it allows you not to over-react or fall into the trap of allowing the person to get the satisfaction of seeing you "lose it". It also allows for you to add detail and better explain yourself.

5. **Compliment the person**: If it is reasonable to do so, thank this person for bringing this to your attention. Talk about the value to the relationship (if there is an established relationship). Show that you respect the person even if you do not agree with him or her or are still angry. Only apologize if you feel as though you are truly sorry and if you really feel that you have done something wrong (whether intentional or not).

Comparing myself with others

It seems to me that at times when I find myself fused with my thoughts, some of my most hurtful thinking happens when I start comparing myself to others. I may be upset that something breaks (and in my experience – everything around me that is expensive tends to all break at once). I have, what some call, "clean suffering", which is the natural result of life. Then, I add to this "clean suffering" some "dirty suffering", which is the product of fusion with thoughts. In this case, it is comparing myself to others: "How come air conditioners, cars, and washing machines don't break all at once – at the same time, for other people? Why is it that I can never afford anything like other people can? Why does everybody else seem to have better jobs, more income, and have fewer problems?" The list of comparisons goes on and before you know it, I may begin to feel sorry for myself. It is then that other people who are around me have to either distance themselves from my negative cloud or join in with me. Usually, I don't get many others to join in my negativity with me. Then, I wonder why they are so happy. It is a challenge for me to pull out of being fused with this type of thinking. There is no doubt that I will probably continue to have this type of thinking, but I don't have to get fused with it every time that it happens.

Accepting my weirdness

I, like many of the clients who I have worked with, have some strange behaviors. I do some things that most NT's don't do (or might not do to the extent that I do). One of those things - is talking to myself, and holding a complete conversation. It is really embarrassing when you don't think other people are around and you are talking to yourself (and responding). Sometimes these conversations are a rehearsal of a past event, a future imagined event, and sometimes just a bunch of gibberish.

Another thing that I have is tics - no not the blood-sucking kind. As long as I can remember, I tend to: suddenly tilt my head, smile fast (a product of pretending to be an NT that became a tic), shrug a shoulder, etc. I also tend to move my leg up and down rapidly, bite my fingers, pace, rock from one foot to another, rock forward and backward, and do "pill rolling" type moves with my fingers, and other things that professionals call "stereotypies". Stereotypies are associated with neurological conditions. Some people think they serve a calming effect in those on the autistic spectrum and have been even called "stims" (for self-stimulation). Anyway, those who don't know about these things will assume that these are conscious behaviors to annoy others - they are not. Anyway, now that I have read much, as well as, talked to clients who have dealt with similar bizarre behaviors, I now understand that this is how I am wired, my neurology - and I accept these things.

Understanding my weirdness

Part of learning to accept my weird, unique, different behaviors was learning to understand that much of my past behaviors could be attributed to neurodiversity.

I was made fun of/picked on, a whole bunch in middle school (or junior high). I now realize it was probably because I didn't act like other kids my age. I probably didn't dress like them, talk like them, and certainly didn't walk like them - literally. I have always had a clumsy awkward walk. When someone was nice to me, for example, a female, I associated any smiles with making fun of me - it was what I expected from experience.

I also had trouble taking things literally, something common for those of us ND's. I remember in college, a girl that I had met while buying books at the college bookstore, had encountered me at a college dance. Actually, I had somehow managed to work up the nerve to go talk to her while she was standing and talking to friends at the dance. After a brief while of talking, she clearly stated "I would like to dance!". I remarked "okay, well - see you later!" and then walked away. Later, someone asked me why I was so rude to her, telling me that she wanted to dance *with me*. My immediate thought was "why didn't she say so?" - as I was clearly under the impression that she wanted to dance, but there was no indication in my mind or communication that it was to be with me. Looking back, I could probably give you thousands of examples when I had taken someone literally.

Not only did I take others literally, but I often had also answered honestly and bluntly when someone has asked me a question. Probably, one reason why I didn't date much nor have dates that stayed with me very long, prior to meeting the woman that I would marry, is probably because I responded honestly to questions like: "Do you like my new haircut?", "Does this dress make my butt look big?", "Are you upset that I spilled my drink in your car?", etc. I will not tell you my responses, but let's just say - I was too honest.

I also realized that my ways of handling stress in the past were not the best, and I have worked so that these ways have changed over the years. When I was very little, when my parents would argue or I was upset, I would curl up in a ball in a closet, behind a bathroom door, or in the shower. Later, I would start talking to myself, pacing, or having a complete "meltdown", which could mean shouting, breaking things, punching walls, etc. Then, as I entered college, it was drowning my fears and anger by drinking alcoholic drinks. As I have become older, my ways of handling stress may unfortunately still involve "meltdowns" but these meltdowns are more internal than external meltdowns. At least now, when I am about to have a meltdown, I am often able to exercise or do something constructive many times. Sometimes, anxiety exhaust me and I have to sleep. Some people may confuse my sleeping with a depressive behavior, but it isn't, it is my body's way of telling me that I am dealing with too much and need to rest some of the anxious energy off.

Alarms and Over-reactions

Whenever I have a meltdown, it is typically due to an over-reaction to an external stimulus (I over-react to things). I would like to say that the more threatening the external thing is, the more that I over-react, but sometimes I interpret a small thing as being a major thing. An example of a common over-reaction: an email from a supervisor asking me why something was done (or done in a timely matter) will set off an alarm telling me that my job or character was in peril. A critical email from the boss could be interpreted as my being horrible at my job, or irresponsible. After receiving such an email, I would become very panic-stricken and often reacted almost like I did as a child, except there was no closet or bathroom to curl up into. I would have to make sure that I still appeared functional to others as to not give anyone an indication that something was wrong with me, after all, I have always been in a position of needing to appear to have everything together so I could function as a therapist and helper to others.

One thing that has helped is using some of the techniques that I discussed earlier such as riding through the waves of anxiety and not doing anything destructive outwardly. I also have a support system of therapy. I believe it is very important when you or on the spectrum or have neuropsychological conditions to have a therapist or neutral professional to guide you.

Some quirky behaviors

Looking back at my childhood, I remember that (in addition to the things from my childhood that I have already mentioned), I have always had many behaviors that NT's may find very strange. These behaviors are part of my high functioning autism. Just so you can read and either relate, understand, or whatever, I have included some examples below:

I have always hated "fuzzy covers" and "scratchy sweaters" - anything woolly or fuzzy (unless it is extremely soft and made of cotton), will be like mini-daggers in my skin.

I don't do well with some noises. If a noise is more than moderately loud, unusual, or annoying to me, I can pretty much go into behaviors ranging from mild irritation to a complete meltdown. I want to say that I am extremely sound sensitive, but not so much anymore as my hearing is now not that great.

I don't like clothing label tags. I can't stand strings or strands of fabric that break free and drag against my skin.

I can't stand fluorescent light (or really any bright light for that matter). My eyes are extremely light sensitive, and I have debated the need to wear sunglasses indoors.

I can be very childlike. I am fascinated with toys, electronic gadgets, and some facts (about galaxies, musicians, etc.). I tend to act childlike sometimes and have always been immature in some ways (around family) but adult-like around strangers.

When I was a child, I preferred talking to adults. Recesses were spent talking to the teacher. When I was young, teachers and doctors would comment how impressed they were with my vocabulary and my level of knowledge of certain topics.

I have some special interests. Some of these have changed over time, but for the things that I am interested in, I research them and become aware of as many facts as I can. I often will bore others talking on and on about some of my favorite subjects. Many times, I am not aware that the other person listening is bored. I sometimes will get the clue when the listener rudely walks away or starts talking to someone else.

I interrupt. As a child, I wasn't aware that I was doing this. As an adult, I sometimes can catch myself after doing it.

I like things to be clean. I tend to have obsessive-compulsive tendencies and do not like germs, dirt, and things that are not in their proper place.

I don't do well with some changes. I like for there to be some predictability and for things to go the way that I think that they logically should.

I prefer to have gadgets with me - they comfort me. I often carry around my tablet, cell phone or any fascinating gadget that I have. For some reason, objects can sometimes soothe me more than people can.

I say things that other people think are funny. The strange thing is that many times I am not really trying to be funny. Words slip out of my mouth. Sometimes I am just being honest. Sometimes I am just letting my internal dialogue slip out.

Some wishes

I wish that there were more jobs that were available for those who think and act differently, like me. I wish more people were educated about people like myself and accepted us. I wish more professionals were able to diagnose these things without the client needing to spend tons of money on lengthy and expensive psychological testing. I wish that there was neurodiversity training and that it would be taken seriously. I also wish that those of you who are reading this, who have not been accepting yourself and your strengths, will now be able to understand that you are not alone, and that you are okay! Again, I don't wish for myself to be cured, but instead, I wish the world was cured of non-acceptance. I was fortunate that I was able to get into a career of helping those who were like myself.

Self-Forgiveness

Not a single one of us is perfect. Furthermore, most of us have things in our "closet" that create shame and times of intense feelings of guilt or remorse.

Part of the recovery process is to be able to be vulnerable.

In this context, being vulnerable means being able to have both self-acceptance (I accept all aspects of myself: the desirable and undesirable) and also to take ownership of our past as well as responsibility for our future.

It is not workable to dwell on everything that we have done wrong. Yet, it also isn't workable to ignore our shortcomings and not try to improve on ourselves.

Recovery Exercise of Forgiveness:

Start out by remembering some things that you have done that you feel bad about. Next, tell your mind with each memory:

"Yes, I did it, and I forgive myself for it."

Or more powerfully say to yourself: "I forgive you."

If it is possible and wouldn't create problems, if you have wronged someone else, just like in a 12 step program, you may consider making amends. Just remember, in order to be gentle to others, you first must learn to be gentle to yourself.

Reaching out to someone that has earned your trust can also help if you need to share some things to someone supportive, someone who will not judge you and will be a symbol of forgiveness.

Remember it -> Own it -> Forgive Yourself -> Challenge yourself to improve in the future.

Ideas for Action:

1. Practice using Assertive Communication: "I think", "I feel", "I would like" (instead of "you always…", "you never").

2. If you don't already have a therapist, contact one and arrange an appointment for individual therapy.

3. Socialize with others who will support you and uplift you and don't isolate – even if you don't feel up to socializing or getting out of bed or the house.

4. Do what the medical professionals tell you: eat right, exercise, get the proper amount of sleep, and take your medications as prescribed.

5. Do some journal writing.

6. Try a support group.

7. Look into spiritually uplifting things or spiritual supports.

8. Reward yourself in healthy ways for healthy behavior or get something that symbolizes your new recovery life.

9. Get back into hobbies or take up new hobbies.

In a nutshell

Accept yourself as you are. When your mind spews forth negativity, recognize this as just "thoughts". For the thoughts that don't move you toward accepting a meaningful life, practice observing that these thoughts are just chatter and don't have to be given power over you. Allow yourself to feel and ride through the waves of emotions without allowing yourself to act-out destructively, numb yourself through drugs or alcohol, or do other isolation or avoidance strategies that will not help you function in the world. Decide to do healthy actions that will give you strength and purpose. Also, find others that you can turn to for support. I wish you the best on your journey!

About the author

Chris L McClish
Current website: https://chrismcclish.com or
Email: chrismcclish@me.com

Chris L McClish, or Christian L McClish, was born in Oklahoma City, Oklahoma, in 1969, as an only child.

As a child, Chris's family moved frequently to different parts of the state of Oklahoma (Oklahoma City, Lake Hefner area, Mustang, and Paul's Valley to name a few places). At the age of nine, his family moved out of Oklahoma to the state of Missouri, where he has resided since.

As a young child, teachers noticed Chris had social issues and processed information differently. He was tested for cognitive issues and the results of which ran contrary to one of his teacher's beliefs (and suggestion to his parents) that he may be "slow", and instead he was revealed to be intellectually gifted. After going from being labeled as "slow" to being seen as highly intelligent (in what seemed like the course of a day), he was encouraged to take part in the "gifted and talented" programs, during his elementary years in Oklahoma.

After his parents and he moved to the town of Peculiar (in approximately the year 1979), there was serious consideration of the school advancing him a grade or two, but at the time the school hadn't done such an advancement before. There was also concern about advancing him because of his social issues, which school administration believed would prevent him from fitting in with older students if they placed him in a higher grade. Due to the school's concerns, he remained in his current grade level.

As a teenager, Chris's father had suffered from both chronic obstructive pulmonary disease (COPD) and progressive dementia (possibly Alzheimer's disease). Due to his father's failing memory and violent mood fluctuations, Chris's father needed to be placed in a skilled care facility. The decision to place his father in an Alzheimer's unit was difficult, as this occurred during Chris's high school years. During that time, Chris's mother's health had also deteriorated, due to her heart and kidney issues. His mother's declining health resulted in Chris having to spend much of his time, outside of school hours, taking care of her.

Marriage and family:

Chris met Stacey Cummings while attending college in Kansas City and married her when he was age 22 (she was 20). Chris's mother died as a result of her health issues shortly before Chris and Stacey's marriage. Chris's father then passed away from complications of dementia two years later, passing away shortly after Chris and Stacey's first child was born.

He currently has three grandchildren from his oldest son'.

Education and Career:

Chris completed high school at Archbishop O'Hara High School in Kansas City. He then obtained both undergraduate and graduate degrees in psychology from Avila University (then called Avila College) in Kansas City. He went on to enjoy a career in the field of counseling, which lasted over 30 years.

In addition to counseling, he participated in mental health advocacy and spent time starting programs/services to help individuals and families cope with the results of mental disorders and addictions. Chris was asked to serve as a topic expert, addressing mental health issues in news and electronic media articles. He was an author of publications both in print and online.

After serving for more than 30 years as a psychotherapist, Chris had retired for five years, and then decided to return to work, and currently works as a Probation and Parole Officer.

Talents, Hobbies, and Skills:

In his teenage years and young adulthood, Chris enjoyed composing music along with playing organ and keyboard (synthesizer) instruments. He participated in music competitions (keyboard and music composition). He also enjoyed playing in a garage band during his high school years and a few years thereafter.

Through his adult years, Chris continued enjoying drawing, painting, and graphic arts. He was regarded by well-known artists for his artistic creations.

Chris also had a natural inclination to be proficient in the use of computers and other technological gadgets.

In his middle-adult years, prior to taking leave due to health issues, Chris served in roles such as; mentor, clinical supervisor, and martial arts coach.

His talents also included wood working (making furniture and items for family members).

Judo: Having studied under great teachers, Chris had gone from someone with no athletic experience (who was bullied in his junior high/ middle school years), into being adept as a martial artist and a martial arts teacher. He attained the rank of Nidan (second degree black belt) in the art. Chris coached both of his sons in addition to serving as a coach for a local Kansas City Judo Club. He became a proponent of a style of Judo/Jujitsu referred to by many names, but more recently as "Empty Gi" (Empty Uniform), which is also referred to as Aiki-Judo (not to be confused with Aikido – which contains more use of wrists and varies in techniques).

Licenses and Certifications:

Chris has been licensed as a certified fitness trainer, a certified life coach, a licensed clinical psychotherapist, a licensed clinical addiction counselor, and has various certifications including in mindfulness meditation instruction. He has served in the past as supervisor, mentor, author, therapist, life coach, coach of Judo, fitness trainer. Because of these roles, he has been referred to by many people as "Teacher", "Sensei", and "Coach".

Experience with Autistic Spectrum Disorders

Many are unaware that both Chris and his youngest son, have been diagnosed as being on the autistic spectrum, both exhibiting mild autism. His oldest son also shows symptoms but was never formally diagnosed. Chris was diagnosed following his youngest son's diagnosis of – what was then called – Asperger's syndrome.

Current Status:

At the time of this writing, he is residing in Peculiar, Missouri with his immediate family.

Also by Chris L McClish

Accepting Life On Life's Terms
Differently Me!

Watch for more at https://www.chrismcclish.com.